£3.5

THESES AND PROJECT WORK

THESES AND PROJECT WORK

A Guide to Research and Writing

C. J. PARSONS

London
GEORGE ALLEN & UNWIN
Boston   Sydney

First published in 1973
Third impression 1980

GEORGE ALLEN & UNWIN LTD
40 Museum Street, London WC1A 1LU

ISBN 0 04 370044 6

Printed in Great Britain by
Hollen Street Press Ltd at Slough

PREFACE

Thesis, extended or long essay, report, dissertation, special study, research paper—these are some of the terms used for the kind of project work that has now become an important part of many diploma and degree courses in further and higher education. All involve students in carrying out research and in submitting the results in an acceptable form.

Project work involves learning several new techniques—systematic research, flexible note-taking, the organization of material on a large scale, disciplined presentation—and, for some time, there has been a need for published advice on these matters. This book is the product of several years' experience of supervising project work and seeks to fulfil that need. Beginning with an explanation of what research of this kind involves, it deals with each stage of the project from the choice of topic to the final presentation.

One word of warning to the student: requirements concerning project work differ widely from one educational establishment to another; consequently no book could attempt to be dogmatic about research of this kind. Instead, what is offered is a guide to basic principles to be used in conjunction with any instructions issued by the tutor (or his department) or by an external examining body.

ACKNOWLEDGEMENTS

I wrote to many universities and polytechnics whilst writing this book and would like to thank those departments who responded with information about the projects carried out on their courses.

I owe a special debt to Nigel Houghton who provided material for several of the chapters in the book and I am very grateful to Miss C. M. Jenkins of the British Standards Institution for allowing me to see the draft of a new standard on the presentation of theses.

I would also like to thank Paul Coulter and Neal Wells for assisting with the chapter on field work; Jack Hughes for making many helpful suggestions; and my wife, Claire, for typing the manuscript.

CONTENTS

CONTENTS

TO THE STUDENT

We have already pointed out in the preface that the material in this book is designed to complement (not to provide a substitute for) any instructions issued by the student's college. In this connection it is particularly important for the student to consult his tutor on the following points:

The topic. The topic of the research must be registered with the establishment. The student is advised to consult with his tutor as fully as possible on this.

Research. The tutor will explain to his student what sort of research he is expected to carry out and how much time and money he should spend.

Length of thesis. The establishment normally lays down a minimum/maximum or approximate length for the thesis.

Form of thesis. The student will have to consult his tutor on such matters as title pages, preface, illustrations, appendixes, etc.; on whether or not chapters should be subdivided; and on such matters as quotations.

Style. The tutor will obviously expect the thesis to be reasonably well written but it is advisable to ascertain whether or not he has any special views on such matters as style and tone.

Documentation. Find out how much documentation is required and what form it should take. Are there any special instructions concerning references and the bibliography?

Presentation. Does the thesis need to be typed and, if it does, on what size of paper? How many copies have to be submitted? Should any of them be bound?

In addition to consulting his tutor on the above points the student should also take the opportunity of looking at any theses which have been accepted in the department in the last few years. Most departments hold copies of a few good theses as examples; alternatively, they may be available for reference at the Library.

I

THE NATURE OF THE TASK

There are many different types of research project and many names for the finished essay: dissertation, thesis, field book, report, special study, extended essay. The names themselves cannot be regarded as a reliable indication of the sort of work involved because they tend to be used rather indiscriminately and are, in fact, virtually synonymous. Obviously, however, not all projects are the same. For example, some are based on research into written sources, others on field work, yet others on experiments carried out in laboratories.

The main differences between the various types of project lie in originality, scope, length and presentation:

Originality. The degree of originality expected is related to the level of the course: the more advanced the course, the more originality is expected. A postgraduate thesis may have to be worthy of publication. At an undergraduate level it may be permissible to present a synthesis of material drawn largely from secondary sources. In postgraduate research the student is expected to rely more heavily on primary sources. Primary sources are poems, novels, letters, newspaper reports, census statistics, tape-recordings, film, diaries, etc. Secondary sources are summaries, interpretations and critiques of primary sources.

Scope of Topic. The more advanced the course, the narrower and hence more specialized will be the field of research and the greater will be the depth of reading and other investigation required.

Length. The length of the dissertation tends to increase in proportion to the originality requirements. The shortest thesis will be about 5,000 words but some undergraduate theses may be as long as 20,000 and a postgraduate thesis could extend to 100,000 words. However, the latter are maximum figures. Length is less important than quality and many excellent theses are relatively short.

Presentation. The more advanced the course, the greater attention the writer will have to pay to detail, especially in documentation; quotations, references and the bibliography will have to be accurate. He will also have to take proportionately more trouble over typing and such matters as binding.

Whatever the level, however, the fundamental purposes of all project work remain the same:

(a) to liberate students from dependence upon course books and lectures.
(b) to cultivate independence of thought and encourage the habit of systematic study.
(c) to develop a student's ability to find, interpret and present material.
(d) to find out whether the student is able to put into practice the principles and theories he has learnt in the course.
(e) to give the student experience of organizing material on a large scale.

Moreover, all theses have features in common which distinguish them from other forms of composition:

Research. Theses embody the results of an investigation. The investigation can be carried out in one of several ways but the method employed is invariably systematic since the aim of the research is to acquire reliable information.

Style. There are certain features of style that tend to distinguish a thesis from other kinds of writing. In .general the writing is formal. There is also the relationship the writer wishes to establish with the reader—that is to say, tone.

Documentation. Theses differ from historical novels and newspaper reports in that the sources of information have to be described fully. In many cases the student will also have to describe the techniques he has used to gather his material.

All project work can be divided into several stages:

(a) Choosing a subject.
(b) Defining the topic. Preliminary reading is required to define the topic. The student will also have discussions with his tutor.
(c) Research and note-taking. This is the major part of the task. In the case of postgraduate work it may take several years.
(d) Organizing the notes.
(e) Writing the first draft.
(f) Submitting all or part of the first draft to tutor. Revision.
(g) Editing the thesis.
(h) Preparing the final version. Getting revised draft typed.
(i) Checking version to be submitted. Binding and submission.
(j) Oral examination.

The rest of this book describes these stages in detail.

The student's tutor may provide him with deadlines for each of the stages. If he does not, the student should devise a realistic timetable for himself.

One last word: writing a thesis may seem an awesome task to anyone undertaking research for the first time; it will involve more work than any other single project on which the student has been engaged before; in addition, the final thesis is probably the longest piece of written work he will ever be asked to produce. However, work of this kind can be very satisfying for several reasons:

If one is interested in the topic, then there is the opportunity to spend a long time on something that is a continuous source of pleasure.

It is satisfying to be able to study a subject in depth instead of having to break off at the very point when one becomes interested.

At the end of the research, one should have a fair claim to be a specialist in one's field and this tends to give one confidence.

A successful thesis can be a very impressive piece of work; it testifies to the fact that a student has the ability to work hard and to analyse a large body of material and this is likely to make a good impression with potential employers.

Research carried on at the undergraduate level can provide the basis for further research in education or industry or possibly pave the way for an academic career.

II

THE TOPIC

1. *The Choice*

There are basically two ways in which one arrives at a topic. Either the tutor (or department) suggests it or one arrives at the choice oneself. There are certain advantages to the first way: the chances are that a topic suggested by one's tutor will be suitable for research and that its scope will be sufficiently limited.

On the other hand, the main pleasure to be derived from research is to immerse oneself in a topic in which one is really interested; if the student finds the subject boring, then the special study will become a millstone around his neck. For this reason, therefore, it is probably better to choose the topic oneself. Usually dissertations are not written until the final year(s) of a course and by that time most students will have developed enthusiasm for some aspect of the work they have been covering.

2. *Pitfalls*

It would be a mistake to suggest that choosing a topic is a simple process. There are many pitfalls to be avoided and there are countless students who have failed to complete their research, not because they were lazy or badly organized, but because their topic was not suitable for research. In this connection it is important for the student to understand that the ultimate responsibility for the choice of topic is his and that, although the tutor may offer advice, he will expect the student to make the final decision.

Probably the most common mistake is to choose a topic that is too large. Before they become fully acquainted with a subject, students are apt to underestimate its dimensions. A business studies student might begin by considering advertising, narrow it down to advertising agencies, and end up with the role of the

17

visualizer. Obviously the breadth of the subject will depend on the level at which the student is working—the lower the level, the broader the subject may be. However, whatever the level, the dissertation is supposed to be a study in depth; this means that it must be far more detailed than other work that the student has undertaken on his course.

Another mistake is choosing a topic which is too complex for research at the level at which the student is studying; in their enthusiasm undergraduates often consider undertaking research that would overawe a Ph.D. student. Obviously, extensive social research, involving large samples and presenting considerable problems in terms of analysis, cannot usually be undertaken by a single undergraduate; ability and experience aside, it is unlikely that he will be able to master the necessary human and mechanical resources for the project.

Time is an important factor. If, for one reason or another, gathering the information will take many months or even years, then this topic is obviously not suitable for an undergraduate student with only a few months in which to complete his project. Unfortunately students often undertake subjects without realizing just how time-consuming they are. This warning is not simply confined to social research topics: for research based on written materials books often have to be borrowed or bought from abroad and this can take a considerable time.

Something else that has to be considered is the accessibility of the material. A postgraduate student may have the time to spend hours in the British Museum and even to travel abroad to examine archives or buildings in foreign countries. But unless he is very lucky the undergraduate student will usually have to confine himself to research based on local sources. Even here, though, there could be problems. A student wishing to do research on the firm or organization for which he works must find out from his employer if there is any information which is too confidential to be included in a project.

Lastly, some topics are simply not researchable at any level. This may be because the sources do not exist; historians occasionally find this is the case since, over the years, many archives have been destroyed or lost. Alternatively, the difficulty may arise because no means has yet been devised for investigating that particular field. Some subjects are so complex—the causes of crime for example—that we are only just beginning to develop techniques for investigating them.

3. *Preliminary Reading*

From what has been said in the previous section it is clear that, apart from consultation with one's tutor, some preliminary work will be required in order to (a) ascertain whether or not the materials for research are available and (b) learn more about the dimensions of the subject so that the student can reduce his topic to manageable proportions. A subject can be narrowed down in a mechanical fashion by taking one of several standard approaches (e.g. the causes of . . . , the consequences of . . . , the methods used in . . . , the various aspects of . . . , the location of . . . , employment in . . .), but this tends to lead to stereotyped projects.

The most effective method of narrowing down a topic is to do some general reading. The college library will probably possess most of the standard reference works (encyclopedias, dictionaries, etc.) in addition to books on the field of study the student has chosen. Simply browsing through these should give the student some insight into the various aspects of his subject and enable him to judge whether or not it can be handled in the time available.

The next step is to draw up a preliminary outline. This should indicate the area of study, the approach to be adopted, and should include the list of any possible source materials already encountered. Of course, at this stage, the outline is bound to be tentative and in no way binds the student. However, it will form the basis of useful discussion with the tutor. In particular, students engaged on field work will need to seek advice at this stage on the feasibility of employing certain methods of social or industrial investigation.

Once this consultation has taken place the student will embark on the major part of his task—the research. There are many kinds of research. Students working in different disciplines will tend to carry out investigation involving different methods. Language, literature and history students tend to rely on written sources;

social science students may use survey methods; geographers and architects tend to rely more on observation and informal interviews. These various types of research are discussed in following chapters, but we must first deal with the techniques of recording information.

III

TAKING NOTES

One of the features of a thesis that distinguishes it from a textbook is that it is documented and that all the sources of information on which it is based are fully acknowledged; sources of information have to be fully described in references, in a bibliography at the end of the thesis, and possibly in the body of the text as well. This means that the results of one's research must be carefully recorded. The method of recording these results will vary with the subject. In some types of research the student will take photographs and make sketches, in others he will use a tape recorder or a note-pad. Whatever the method and the source, he should begin by recording full details of the source itself before he has even had time to assess its relevance. In this way he will ensure that he never finds himself with information whose source he cannot trace.

There is no standard way of describing non-written sources such as people or television programmes and it is up to the student to devise his own way. What is important is that the description should be as full as possible and that the same sort of information should be recorded for each source of that kind. In such matters consistency is particularly important. With written sources, however, the case is different. There is a widely accepted way of describing published and unpublished material and the student will probably be expected to adhere to this.

The most popular method of taking notes from written sources is on record cards because they have several important advantages. They are tougher and will withstand handling over a period of time without becoming damaged. They are also compact, easy to handle, and can be stored conveniently in purpose-built boxes. Most important, a card system is flexible: cards are easy to arrange and rearrange, to group and classify, and this is an enormous advantage when the student is faced with the task of writing up his notes. However, if the system is to retain its flexibility the student must put only one note on each card. If he breaks this rule, then he may as well be using quarto or foolscap paper.

Record cards can be bought in three sizes: 5″ × 3″, 6″ × 4″, 8″ × 5″. It is, perhaps, wise to avoid the largest size since it may encourage the tendency to put too much material on one card.

As with other types of source the notes you take will fall into two groups: information about the source (bibliographical information) and notes from the body of the text. You should make a separate set of cards for each and they should be kept apart; it is quite usual for students to use different sizes for each purpose: 5″ × 3″ cards for bibliographical information and 6″ × 4″ for notes from the text. Once you have chosen a size of card for a particular purpose keep to that size; it is easy to lose a 5″ × 3″ card in a collection of 6″ × 4″ cards.

1. *Source Cards*

Bibliographical information should be taken down from the source itself. If the source does not provide all the information needed, then the student should look for it on the library catalogue card. Any information that has to be obtained from the catalogue should be placed in square brackets. Write down each piece of information on a separate line.

For books record the following information in this order:

(a) *Name of author(s) or issuing body.* This should be taken down exactly as it appears on the title page.

Where a work has three or more authors, the abbreviation 'et al.' meaning 'and others' can be used for the second and subsequent names:

James G. McManaway *et al.*

If the author writes under a pseudonym this should be placed first, followed by the author's real name in square brackets. If the work was published anonymously and the author's name is

22

not known, then the abbreviation 'Anon' should be used. In the case of anonymous publications where the author's name is known, it should be included in the normal way but placed in square brackets:

[Peter Whalley] *Essay* . . .

Where a work originally appeared under the author's initials the name should be completed in square brackets:

D[erwent] C[oleridge]

When publications have editors rather than authors the name(s) should be noted followed by the abbreviation 'ed':

Hugh Fraser and W. R. O'Donnell, eds.

Where the author is an institution the name of the establishment should be recorded:

Central Office of Information, *Britain: an Official Handbook,* . . .

(b) *Title.* The title of the publication should normally be recorded in full, together with any subtitles, and underlined. Only long titles and the titles of well-known works such as classics should be abbreviated. If you are consulting individual articles in a collection or an encyclopedia, record the article title in quotation marks before the collection title:

Hugh Fraser, 'The Teaching of Writing', *Linguistic.* . . .

(c) *Editor/translator.* Where someone's work has been edited or translated the names of those responsible should be recorded. It is usual to use the abbreviations 'ed.' (edited by) and 'trans.' (translated by).

(d) *The edition.* The edition should be recorded if the work is in its second or subsequent edition: **2nd edn.** The printing history of a book is normally recorded on the reverse of the title page.

(e) *Volumes.* With multi-volume publications note the total number of volumes: **4 vols.**

23

(f) *Place of publication.* Normally the town is sufficient but where there is more than one town of the same name (Cambridge, Massachussetts and Cambridge, England) or the place is not well known (Menasha, Wisconsin or Harmondsworth, Middlesex) it may be necessary to record the state, county or country as well. Some people take the view that the place need not be mentioned if it is London, England. When the place of publication is not known use the abbreviation 'n.p.'. Where several places of publication are given, record the first.

(g) *Publisher.* Not all establishments expect the publisher to be cited. Ask your tutor about this.

(h) *Date of publication.* Record the date of the edition (not the reprint date). For multivolume publications issued over several years, record the inclusive dates of publication: **1967–71.**

(i) *Volume number.* If you are not using all the volumes in a multi-volume publication, record in upper-case roman numerals the volume(s) you are consulting: **XIV.**

(j) *Page numbers.* With articles in collections or encyclopedias, record the pages the article occupies: **121–139.**

For serial publications (journals, newspapers, magazines) record the following:

(a) *Author or issuing body.*

(b) *Title of article.* This should be placed in single quotation marks. For quotations within the title, use double marks.

(c) *Title of publication.* This should be recorded in full unless there is a recognized standard abbreviation (see BS 4148).

(d) *Volume number.* This is recorded in upper case roman numerals.

(e) *Date of publication.* The full date is required for daily and weekly publications. Otherwise it is usual to give just the month and year.

(f) *Page numbers.* Record the page(s) which the article occupies: **177–192.**

For manuscripts record the author, title (in inverted commas), the collection (underlined), and manuscript number.

The student is referred to Nokes* for the method in which to cite the following:

Acts of parliament
Statutory instruments
Bills
Parliamentary proceedings
Decisions

For theses the following details should be recorded in this order:

(a) Author's name in the form in which it appears on the title page.

(b) Full title. Place this in quotation marks.

(c) The course or degree.

(d) The name of the university.

(e) Year in which it was accepted.

In the case of all sources consulted in libraries, museums, etc., the student should note the name of the establishment on the reverse of his source card. This information is not usually included in the thesis but it is useful for future reference. For the same reason the student should also record the classification number.

2. *Note Cards*

On the note cards the following will be recorded:

(a) In the top right-hand corner of the card, the surname of the author *or* the name of the issuing body *or*—if the source was published anonymously—a short title. If you are consulting several works by a single author, use a short title as well:

Hanson, *Textbook*, p. 77.

* G. D. Nokes, *Manual of Legal Citations*, University of London Institute of Advanced Legal Studies, 2 vols, London, 1959–60.

25

SOURCE CARD   ARTICLE

> A. Shaw
> 'Student Welfare — Cause
> for Concern'
> The Technical Journal
> IX June 1971
> 22–25

SOURCE CARD   BOOK

> C. A. Moser
> Survey Methods in Social
> Investigation
> Heinemann
> London
> 1958

SOURCE CARD   THESIS

Samuel John Hughes
'The Early Browning (1812-1840)'
Ph. D. thesis
University of London
1966

SOURCE CARD   MANUSCRIPT

Thomas Birch
[Abstract of] 'Dr Swift's History
of the last Parliament of
Queen Anne'
British Museum: Additional
4253 (54)   Manuscripts

NOTE CARD   SUMMARY FROM ARTICLE

> student counselling   Shaw, .23
>
> The importance of student
> counselling has been recognised
> in France and the U.S.A.
> for some time.

NOTE CARD   QUOTATION FROM BOOK

> purpose of surveys   Moser, p.2
>
> 'The purpose of many surveys
> is simply to provide someone
> with information.'

This information is the key to the source card.

(b) After the key, write the precise part of the source from which the information was drawn. With multi-volume publications (books) note first the number of the volume you are using. Following this will be the page, line, or column which should be recorded in the same form as it appears in the source.

With single-volume publications the page number should be preceded by the abbreviation 'p.' (or 'pp.' where more than one page is involved: **pp. 178–179**), but in the case of multi-volume and serial publications this is usually omitted: **I, 88.**

Some early publications had pages without numbers: instead, the right-hand pages were lettered A, B, C, etc. In these cases use the letter followed by a small r (recto) for the right-hand page and the same letter followed by a small v (verso) for the following left-hand page.

With references to the Bible record the chapter and verse in arabic numerals and separate them by a colon:

Genesis 2:3.

With plays note the act, scene and line:

Macbeth III, i, 5.

If poems are written in books, cantos, verses, etc., these must be included in the reference. Use upper-case roman numerals for books, lower-case for cantos or verses and arabic numerals for the line. The abbreviations l. and ll. (lines) should be used for lines in a single-volume publication without subdivision. In the case of multi-volume publications and single-volume publications with subdivisions the line should stand by itself:

***Faerie Queen*, IV, xxv, 23** not **line 23** or **l. 23.**

When referring to columns in tables use arabic numerals: **Col. 4.**

When you are noting material occupying several pages or lines record the inclusive numbers instead of using abbreviations such as 'et. seq.' (and the following pages).

(c) In the top left-hand corner write a word or phrase that indicates the subject-matter of the note. This will save time when you come to sort through the notes.

(d) Use the centre of the card for the note. Most of the student's notes will take the form of paraphrases of the original. This is because there are only a few restricted circumstances in which it is desirable to quote the actual words of the source. Care must be taken not to misrepresent the meaning of the original passage. In the case of complex material it is probably wise to photocopy it so that one can paraphrase it at leisure; photocopying is now relatively cheap and can therefore be used quite extensively. The student will find it desirable to quote rather than to paraphrase his source in the following circumstances:

(i) Where the author has expressed something in a particularly apt or telling fashion.
(ii) Where the author's words as well as his ideas are under discussion.
(iii) Where the words of the source are likely to lend authority to your argument.

All quoted material must be placed in inverted commas so that there is no risk of mistaking it for a paraphrase or vice versa. The spelling and punctuation of the original must be recorded with scrupulous accuracy; inaccurate quotations are a mark of unsound scholarship and could lead to the rejection of the thesis. Any omissions the student makes must be indicated by three dots, or four dots if parts of more than one sentence have been left out. However, omissions must not be made that alter the meaning of the original. Any insertions which the student thinks are necessary to clarify the meaning of the original must be placed in square brackets:

'He asked the Treasurer [Harley] to call that evening.'

Where there is an apparent inaccuracy in the original the student can indicate that it is the author's, not his own, by inserting *sic* in brackets after the word or passage in question:

'He asked Swite [*sic*] if he had written *Gulliver's Travels.*'

30

This chapter has been concerned with use of the card system in note-taking from written sources but it should be clear that the advantages of this system will also make it a useful technique of recording information from other types of sources such as radio programmes, informal interviews where no interview schedule is used, or for recording observations made on field studies.

IV

RESEARCH—WRITTEN SOURCES

Most students will at some time have to visit one or more libraries during the course of their research. Even if the bulk of his research is field work the student will still need to use the library for preliminary reading and, in addition, his tutor may require that he make himself familiar with any published material relating to his topic.

Much material can be located simply by browsing on the shelves or through the catalogue of a good library. However, this is not a particularly efficient method of locating written sources of information. The quickest and most effective way is to consult the major bibliographies, most of which should be in your college library. What follows is a select list of such bibliographies. All are useful and each should be consulted. Subject bibliographies have not been included as these can be found in several of the bibliographies *of* bibliographies.

Constance Winchell, *Guide to Reference Books*, 8th edition, Chicago, 1967.

Divided into five sections:

General Reference Works
The Humanities
The Social Sciences
History and Area Studies
Pure and Applied Sciences

Within each of these major sections there are subject divisions. For each subject Winchell gives the relevant encyclopedias, dictionaries, indexes and bibliographies. Each entry is fully annotated. The first section (General Reference Works) lists guides to manuscripts, newspapers, government publications, dissertations and geneology. Part C (The Social Sciences) contains a useful section on sources of statistical information for many countries. A Supplement was issued in 1968.

A. J. Walford, *Guide to Reference Material*, 2nd edition, 3 vols, London, 1966–70.
Arranged according to the Universal Decimal Classification System it includes subject encyclopedias and bibliographies, directories and guides to periodicals. Volume I covers science and technology and has a useful section for management students. Volume II is devoted to philosophy, psychology, religion, sociology, geography and biography. It contains a useful section on maps and also lists sources of statistical information for many countries. Volume III covers the arts and literature. Most of the material cited in Walford is British but foreign publications are included.

Robert L. Collison, *Bibliographies Subject and National: A Guide to their Content, Arrangement and Use*, 3rd edition, London, 1968.
The first and larger part lists bibliographies in, among other fields, philosophy, psychology, theology, language and literature, geography, history, the social sciences and the arts. The second part includes universal bibliographies, national bibliographies (Great Britain, United States, France and Germany only), bibliographies of bibliographies, and lists of serial publications. It is fairly compact but is a very useful place to begin one's research.

G. Chandler, *How to Find Out: A Guide to Sources of Information for All Arranged by the Dewey Decimal Classification*, 3rd edition, London, 1967.
This lists the major subject bibliographies in each field. It also contains a useful section on unpublished sources of information.

William A. Bagley, *Facts and How to Find Them: A Guide to Sources of Information and to the Method of Systematic Research*, 7th edition, London, 1964.
Written for the layman but containing useful chapters on bibliographies of bibliographies, 'official' publications, MS sources, local history and 'other sources of information'.

Theodore Besterman, *A World Bibliography of Bibliographies and Bibliographical Catalogues, Calendars, Abstracts, Digests, Indexes and the Like*, 4th edition, 5 vols. Lausanne, 1965–66.
This has an alphabetical arrangement by subject. Large subject sections are subdivided: within these subdivisions the arrangement is chronological. Volume V is a combined author and title index. Altogether about 117,000 bibliographies are listed under 16,000 subject headings. Apart from looking under his particular subject the student should consult the section on 'Bibliography' which lists bibliographies of bibliographies, bibliographies of periodicals (including abstracting and indexing services), bibliographies of national bibliographies, etc.

Bibliographic Index, H. W. Wilson Co., New York. Issued monthly. Until 1951 there were quarterly and yearly cumulations; since then cumulations have been semi-annual and biannual.
The arrangement is by subject: under each subject publications are listed in alphabetical sequence, books and pamphlets by author, periodicals by title. It is to be regarded as supplementary to Besterman but essential for those years not yet covered by Besterman, i.e. 1963 onwards.

Cumulative Book Index, H. W. Wilson Co., New York. Issued monthly, with yearly, bi-annual and five-year cumulations.
A guide to books published in the English language (covers Britain, Canada, United States and other countries). The arrangement is by country. Under each country, subjects and books are listed in a single alphabetical sequence; each publication is included twice—under its subject and under its author (or title if it has no author).

British National Bibliography. A weekly guide to British publications, first issued in 1950.
It is arranged according to Dewey. A subject and author index is published each month but the student will probably find it most useful to consult the yearly cumulations.

Government Publications, H.M.S.O.
A guide to the publications of the various British government departments and sections; it is useful as these are not included in

the *British National Bibliography*. Issued daily, monthly, and annually, it has a consolidated index published every five years. Students may also need to consult the sectional lists covering the publications of individual departments in greater detail.

Monthly Catalogue: United States Public Documents. United States of America Government Printing Office, Washington. Equivalent of above for the United States of America.

Ulrich's International Periodicals Directory, ed. Marietta Chicorel, 12th edition, 2 vols, New York, 1967–68.
As its title indicates this directory does not restrict itself to the publications of any one country. Volume II is devoted to the arts, humanities, business and social science. A Supplement to both volumes was issued in 1969. Subjects are arranged alphabetically. At the beginning of each volume there is an alphabetical list of the abstracting and indexing services covering the relevant fields. Students looking for sources of statistical information will find the section on statistics particularly useful.

British Union-Catalogue of Periodicals: A Record of the Periodicals of the World, from the Seventeenth Century to the Present Day, in British Libraries, ed. James D. Stewart, Muriel E. Hammond and Erwin Saenger, 4 vols, London, 1955–58.
Alphabetical arrangement. This covers periodicals of all nationalities and gives details of period of issue and where periodicals are held. A Supplement was issued in 1962. Since then *New Periodical Titles* has been issued quarterly with annual cumulations.

Guide to Current British Periodicals, ed. Mary Toase, London, 1962.
Arranged according to Dewey. It tells the student which periodicals are covered by an indexing service. It also contains an appended list of abstracting journals.

Index to Theses Accepted for Higher Degrees in the Universities of Great Britain and Ireland, Aslib. Issued annually since 1950.
Arranged under subjects, with an author index. Not all universities will lend theses to other universities. Details of loan facilities can be found at the beginning of Volume XVI.

Guide to Unpublished Research Materials, ed. Ronald Staveley, London, 1957.
Half this book is devoted to the social sciences and includes sections on statistical material, sources in market research and sources in sociology and psychology.

Historical Manuscripts Commission, *Record Repositories in Great Britain*, 3rd edition, London, 1968.
Repositories are listed under towns and there is an index of institutions at the back. The guide does not record what each repository contains but it does give circumstances in which they can be visited. The student may also find a use for Hubert Hall's *Repertory of British Archives Part I: England*, London, 1920. The contents of the Public Record Office are described in a three-volume guide published by Her Majesty's Stationery Office.

D. W. Humphreys and F. G. Emmison, *Local History for Students*, London, 1967.
This includes sections on local collections, county and parish estate and manorial records.

Lester K. Born, *Unpublished Bibliographical Tools in Certain Archives and Libraries of Europe*, Washington, 1952.

Historical Manuscripts Commission, *Guide to the Reports of the Royal Commission on Historical Manuscripts*. In two parts.
The first is a topographical guide published in 1914; the second an index of persons (1938 and 1966).

Aslib Directory: A Guide to Sources of Information in Great Britain and Ireland, ed. Miriam Alman, 2 vols, London 1957.
Volume II is a directory of libraries and information services. The arrangement is according to town and there is a regional index listing libraries under counties. Volume I is a subject guide arranged according to the Universal Decimal Classification system and it also contains an alphabetical subject index. Altogether some 3,000 sources are listed, including national, university, public and county libraries, museums, cathedrals, embassies, hospitals and firms. In each case details are given of the scope of the collection, the catalogue, opening times and circumstances in which material is lent. Volume II of a new edition

was published in 1968. This covers science, technology and commerce.

British Museum: the General Catalogue of Printed Books
At some stage in their research most students visit one of Britain's national libraries. Of these the most frequently used is the British Museum which has a stock of over six million volumes. For details of its catalogues see *Aslib Directory*, II, 441. The author catalogue is published in book form and can usually be found in universities and larger public libraries. All periodicals are listed under P (for Periodicals), then by place of publication. University publications are listed under their country of origin.

G. P. Henderson and I. G. Anderson, *Current British Directories*, 6th edition, Beckenham, Kent, 1970.
This is divided into four parts: local, specialized, international, and commonwealth directories. It includes everything from the *Kennel Club: Calendar and Stud Book* to the *European Computer Users Handbook*. Each directory gives information about people and organizations in the particular industry, trade or group. Altogether a very useful guide to unpublished sources of information. Students particularly concerned with professional societies and associations should look at *The Directory of British Associations*, 3rd edition, Beckenham, Kent, 1970.

Students may also find use for *Councils, Committees and Boards*, Beckenham, Kent, 1970.

Whenever you find a source which you think may be of interest, record its details in the manner described in Chapter III. In this way you will build up what is called a 'working bibliography' or reading list. In assessing the value of material collected from written sources the student should keep the following in mind:

Eyewitness accounts. Accounts by eyewitnesses (diaries, memoirs, correspondence, autobiographies, newspaper reports) and participants are apt to be biased. In 1971 Harold Wilson and George Brown published different accounts of Brown's resignation from the Labour Government. Sources may also need to be authenticated. This problem arose with the publication in the Western world of what were claimed to be Kruschev's memoirs.

Technical information. This should be up to date. Make sure you consult the most recent edition available of the book in question. Also check the status of the author and publisher.

Statistics. These can easily be misused or misinterpreted. Take particular care over headings to statistical tables; these should be reproduced faithfully.

Translations. Try to find out which is the most reliable translation available. In some circumstances the best translation may not be the most appropriate. If, for example, you are discussing Fielding's interest in Rabelais it is probably better to use a contemporary translation of Rabelais rather than a modern one.

Edition. In the case of plays, poetry, novels, etc., there are usually standard editions. The student should make sure these are the ones he uses.

V

FIELD WORK

In this chapter we will be concerned with what is known as field work. This type of research is difficult to undertake without special training and in a book of this length there is not enough space to deal with the subject in detail. However, some attempt will be made to describe the main kinds of field work and some of the problems involved in each.

Field work varies mainly in the degree to which the observer controls the situation he is investigating and in the extent to which he participates in that situation or, in the case of social research, interacts with the subjects under investigation. The sort of research a student carries out will depend on the nature of his subject and the amount of time, help and equipment he has at his disposal. Another factor will be the extent to which he wishes to generalize on the basis of his findings. Some investigations, such as case studies, may involve a combination of several different research methods.

1. *Sampling*

In most cases it is not practical to look at every object or question every person involved in the situation one is investigating. Therefore the investigator has to work with a sample. The usefulness of the findings of his research will depend largely on the extent to which the sample is genuinely *representative*. Ideally the sample should contain various types in the same proportion as they occur in the total number under investigation. One begins sampling by establishing the 'sampling frame', that is to say, by defining the total number of objects or people under investigation.

Obtaining a complete list sometimes presents problems. Many

useful sources of information are, for various reasons, unwilling to co-operate. Some lists such as directories are published and are easily available.* For some types of research electoral registers or local authority rating rolls can be used. In other cases various organizations may be approached. There are firms who provide circulation lists for a fee. Other useful sources of information will be the town hall (for local organizations), and local government officers (for example, the Medical Officer of Health holds a list of buildings covered by the factory acts). However, certain types of people, such as tramps and criminals, may always be difficult to locate.

There are several different types of sampling:

(a) *Random sampling*. This is the easiest method of sampling. It involves a lottery method where numbers are 'picked out of a hat'. For example, the names of all the people in the population could be numbered and then a sample chosen by using tables of random numbers. The value of this method is that each person in the sampling population stands an equal chance of being selected. However, it follows from this that random sampling does not ensure that the various types of person in the population will be represented proportionately.

(b) *Stratification*. This is used when one knows that the total number under investigation consists of homogeneous subgroups. If one knew, for example, that there were only 2,000 women in a population of 10,000, one could create two subgroups (one for each sex) and take a proportionate random sample from each; for a sample of 100, 80 would be taken from the male group, 20 from the female. This would avoid the danger of disproportionate female representation involved in purely random sampling.

(c) *Quota sampling*. With all types of random sampling it is essential that each person represented by a chosen number is visited; as soon as one substitutes other numbers the sample is no longer random. This means that the investigator may have to call back several times to contact subjects, which can be time-

* See G. P. Henderson and I. G. Anderson, *Current British Directories*, 6th edition, Beckenham, Kent, 1970.

consuming. If the 'no contacts' amount to as high as 10 per cent of the sample, the findings of the research are no longer valid. For these reasons, much research is based on quota sampling.

With this method the population is stratified according to sex, age, class, etc., and a sample from each sub-group is taken. This is very often done by stopping people in the street who appear to 'fit the bill'. Statisticians are apt to point out that in practice quota samples are less representative than random samples. One problem is that interviewers often station themselves in places where they are unlikely to encounter people representative of their sub-group. However, the main problem is that one has to know a considerable amount about the population (age, status, sex) before one can devise satisfactory quotas. On the other hand it should be said that one of the greatest setbacks in survey work —a low response—is more easily overcome with quota samples; the student simply finds another person in the appropriate sub-group.

The final consideration in sampling is the size of the sample to be taken. Obviously most investigators would prefer to use a small sample since much less work is involved. However, a small sample can really be used only where all the subjects in the research are known to have a large number of characteristics in common. In most instances, of course, this will not be the case. In general the larger the sample the more reliable the results are likely to be.

2. *Observation.*

Most field work involves observing people or objects and/or asking questions. Of the two techniques observation is probably the more widely used. Some types of research, such as field studies carried out by architecture, geography or town-planning students, may rely exclusively on this method. Usually some kind of field book is used for recording notes but with investigation into such areas as traffic movement it is advisable to devise a schedule (a form with spaces for recording observations).

One problem with this method of research is that human observation is known to be unreliable; we tend to bring our own prejudices and a tendency to select what suits us to every situation; what we see and what we think we see are often very different. For this reason film and/or a tape-recorder are often used. Another problem which arises with research into people is that human beings tend to behave untypically when they know they are being watched. For this reason some researchers have gone to unusual lengths to conceal their presence, employing such devices as two-way mirrors and hidden cameras. However, these methods can only be used where the investigator controls the environment of the research.

Some types of investigation involve mixing with the subjects. This is sometimes called 'action research'. Examples of this would include going to work in a factory or an office or joining a community or a group to observe the behaviour of people at close hand over a fairly long period. The investigator may ask the people questions but, wherever possible, he tries not to draw attention to himself so that his presence does not cause the subjects to behave in an untypical manner. Indeed some investigators have felt it necessary to disguise themselves, changing not only their clothes but their whole demeanour. Naturally, in these circumstances, note-taking tends to be a problem; observations may have to be recorded surreptitiously on scraps of paper! Alternatively a concealed tape-recorder may be used.

3. *Interviews*

Research students use both formal and informal interview techniques. We have already mentioned informal interviews in connection with 'action research' but this technique of gaining information is likely to be used in many different circumstances. In most cases the student will begin the interview with a few prepared questions but will then follow what promise to be fruitful avenues of enquiry, feeling his way as he goes. This kind of investigation requires considerable skill and tact. The interviewer should try to put his subject at ease so that he does not feel he is being interrogated. Conventional note-taking may not be possible in such circumstances, in which case the student may want to use a tape-recorder. However, permission to do this should be obtained beforehand.

Plenty of time must be allowed to process the results of this kind of research; as the subjects in the investigation are not answering standard questions the responses will take much longer to analyse.

With survey work more formal techniques are used. Each person in the sample answers the same questions in the same order; the questions form a standard list on what is known as an interview 'schedule'. Wherever possible the questions are provided with a set of alternative answers so that the interviewer ticks one of a series of boxes rather than writing out an answer:

Which daily papers have you bought during the last week?

Daily Express	*Daily Telegraph*
Guardian	*The Times*
The Globe	*Sun*
Daily Mail	*Morning Star*
Daily Mirror	

This makes the findings much easier to analyse.

One danger with these schedules is that none of the answers may be the right one and that the interviewee may find himself giving an answer that is not his own. There are two ways of overcoming this problem. One is to carry out a pilot survey, that is, to use the schedule on a small group so that revisions can be made before the sample is interviewed. The other is to provide a space entitled 'Other Answers' at the end of each list of possible responses.

The questions themselves will fall into one of two broad categories. First, all surveys—even opinion polls—usually contain some factual questions on such matters as the interviewee's age, sex, occupation, etc.:

Are you	**under 25**	**25–39**
	40–55	**over 55**

These are usually placed at the beginning of the schedule. Factual questions are included so that an analysis can take into account any correlations between, for example, age and political attitudes. Questions may also be included to discover the extent of the interviewee's knowledge of the subject under investigation. For example, in a survey on political attitudes, a factual question

43

such as 'which of the following is Home Secretary?' may precede a question calling for an assessment of the Home Secretary's image. Questions on subjects about which the interviewee may be sensitive (e.g. income) should be left to the end of the schedule.

The second type of question calls for the expression of opinions or attitudes. These questions often begin with such words as 'Which of the following attitudes to . . . most closely resembles your own . . . ?' followed by a series of sentences, words, or phrases, each expressing a different opinion or attitude:

Which two of the following words or phrases do you think best apply to *The Globe*?

young person's paper	intellectual
forthright	old person's paper
entertaining	has integrity
comprehensive	controversial
upper-class	thorough
staid	establishment

Attitude questions may be concerned with eliciting information about the strength of people's feelings. In these cases, answers of varying degrees of intensity are provided:

What would you feel if *The Globe* ceased publication tomorrow?

very sorry	glad
sorry	very glad
indifferent	

To learn more about people's feelings on such subjects as race, special scales have been devised. For further details on these the student is referred to the book by Peter Mann listed in the bibliography.

The following general points should be made about interview schedules. First, they should contain as few questions as possible: if the interviewee becomes bored he is likely to answer questions inaccurately or not to tell the truth. Second, they should only contain questions that are *likely* to be answered accurately; questions that are too difficult or that may cause embarrassment will probably not be answered faithfully. Third, a great deal of thought must be given to the wording of the questions; it is surprising how easy it is to phrase a question in such a way that it is ambiguous or confusing. Fourth, some thought has to be given to the sequence of the questions; the order in which they are asked should appear to make sense.

The best way to avoid these difficulties is, as we have said elsewhere, to carry out a pilot survey with a small group. This should bring out any weaknesses in the design of the schedule which can then be revised before it is used with your sample.

4. *Postal Questionnaires*

Most of what has been said about interview schedules is true of postal questionnaires. Each of the two techniques has its advantages. The main advantage of the interview is that the interviewer may be able to overcome any reluctance on the part of the interviewee to answer some of the questions. In addition the interviewer can do his best to ensure that everyone in the sample does in fact respond; the greatest disadvantage to postal questionnaires is that many people do not return them. On the other hand it should be pointed out that there is a danger the interviewer's tone of voice can influence the response of the subject. Finally, postal questionnaires can save considerable time and effort.

If the student does use postal questionnaires he should give some thought to their design. Ideally they should be printed (rather than duplicated) on good quality paper. A covering letter should be sent explaining the purpose of the research and asking for co-operation. Also, if a stamped, addressed envelope is enclosed the response is likely to be much higher.

5. *Analysing Answers*

With all types of research the student has to be concerned with the reliability of his findings and this is especially the case with survey work where bias can enter in many different ways. Some possible sources of bias can be eliminated in the planning stage when the questions are designed and the sample chosen; we have already pointed out in earlier sections some of the difficulties that arise in designing schedules and questionnaires. It is necessary to stress the importance of careful planning in survey work since it is very difficult to identify bias in the answers to surveys. All the student can look for are obvious inconsistencies or gaps in the responses; if these are present it may be necessary to go back to the person involved for clarification.

Even when the sample is chosen carefully there will be what is called a 'sampling error' because the sample will not represent the population exactly. One of the advantages of random—as opposed to quota—sampling is that the probability of error can be more easily calculated.

A large number of non-responses will affect the value of the findings. With quota sampling it may be possible to find other people who 'fit the bill' but with random sampling it will probably be necessary to treat non-respondents in the same way as respondents; that is, to assume that they would have answered each question in the same way as the majority of respondents.

There are various ways of tabulating the responses. In the case of surveys, like the population census involving very large numbers, computers are used. With other large surveys data processing machines are used. If this equipment is not available at the student's establishment then he will have to tabulate by hand. He does this by designing a large 'chart' on which there are labelled boxes for each of the possible responses. He then works

Under 25	25–29	30–39	40–55	Over 55
XXXXXX	XXXXXX			
XXXXXX	XXXXXX			
XXXXXX				

his way through the completed forms, indicating the responses by ticks or crosses in the appropriate boxes. When he has entered the result of the last form he counts up the entries in each box.

What will the student do with these numbers? First, he is usually interested in how many own/do/think, etc. this and how many own/do/think, etc. that. Usually the figures involved are represented as percentages but this should not be done if the sample was small (less than 100).

The student may also want to calculate the mean, mode and median for each question. The mean is the arithmetic average, the mode the figure that occurs most frequently, and the median the middle figure in a series arranged in order of importance. The difference is most clearly illustrated if we take a survey on earnings in which, out of a sample of 1,000, 400 earned £10 a week and 600 earned £15 a week; the mean would be £12 but the median and the mode are £15.

Third, the student will be concerned with relationships between sets of figures. He may note, for example, that 73 per cent of the respondents over 50 used the 'Nell Gwynne Tea Rooms' at least three times a week or that 63 per cent of the respondents who smoked at least ten cigarettes a day had three or more children. Such information is interesting but, obviously, the student has to be very careful about suggesting any kind of causal relationship in these cases; the figures should be seen mainly as suggesting possible areas for future research.

For further information on analysis and other aspects of field work, the student is referred to the books by Mann, Moser and Madge listed in the bibliography. The next chapter will take up more general matters of organization.

VI

ORGANIZING MATERIAL

1. *The Parts of a Thesis*

A thesis may contain the following parts in this order:

(a) Title page
(b) Table of contents
(c) Acknowledgements. Any help received in the provision of facilities should be acknowledged. Students may also use this section to record a special debt to a particular source.
(d) Abstract (synopsis)
(e) List of abbreviations: the abbreviated titles used in footnotes
(f) List of tables
(g) List of illustrations
(h) Body of thesis, divided into chapters
(i) Appendixes
(j) List of references (if these have not been given on the relevant pages)
(k) Bibliography. This may be divided into sections, e.g. MSS, primary and secondary sources; published—unpublished.

At this stage the student need not concern himself with most of these parts. This chapter is concerned solely with the content and arrangement of the body of the thesis and with the circumstances in which it is desirable to relegate material to an appendix.

2. *Selecting Material*

During the course of his research the student may have taken several thousand notes. He must now be prepared to discard much of this material; a thesis must be closely argued and no irrelevant material should be retained simply because it has been collected. He should bear in mind at this stage, and also when he is writing the thesis, that he is addressing a specialist audience and not the general public.

The student will now find how useful the subject headings are on the notes since they obviate the necessity for reading through all the material he has assembled. When he has sifted through the notes he may find that he has rejected more than he has retained. This is not unusual. However, he should not throw away the rejected material since it could easily prove useful at another time. The decision as to what illustrative material should be used can probably be postponed for the moment.

3. *Arranging material*

Like most other types of composition a thesis should have a beginning, middle, and an end. The beginning should take the form of an introduction or an introductory chapter. This section is normally used for the following purposes:

(a) To state precisely the area of research. In some respects a clear statement of aims is in the student's own interest since he can hardly be censured for failing to cover something outside the terms of reference. This is the most important function this section serves.

(b) To explain why the research was carried out.

(c) To draw attention to the original nature of the findings and/or its conclusions.

(d) To draw attention to the inadequacy of work that has so far been carried out in this field. As readers of *Lucky Jim* may recall it is usual to refer to the subject of one's thesis as 'this strangely neglected topic'.

(e) To describe the method of research if this is particularly unusual or important. With social sciences, where the method of investigation is particularly important, a large section of the thesis might be devoted to this.

(f) To mention any special difficulties that have been encountered during the course of the research.

At the end of the thesis, there should be a conclusion or concluding chapter in which the main points are drawn together. Here, as at the beginning of the thesis, the student will want to draw attention to the importance of his findings. With certain types of research he may also want to make suggestions or recommendations. In addition, this section may indicate what work still remains to be done in this or closely related fields.

As far as the body of the thesis is concerned, there are several standard ways of approaching a subject:

(a) A detailed examination of an event, poem, individual organization or theory.

(b) A comparison in which likenesses and differences are pointed out: two areas, two writers, practice and theory in a particular field of enquiry.

(c) Setting up arguments ('straw men') and knocking them down point by point; reconstructing a traditional or a superficial view and demolishing it. However, such an approach should not appear merely iconoclastic.

These can involve one or more standard arrangements:

A chronological arrangement. This is suitable wherever time is an important feature of the subject-matter. This disposition is suitable for historical subjects, discussion of a series of poems or of the various stages in which the poem was composed, or the description of a series of experiments or investigations.

Order by space. This arrangement is conventional in theses which discuss the individual parts of a whole and would be suitable for the treatment of the different parts of a geographical region, town or building, or the structure of an organization. Each part would be placed according to its relation to the other parts so that there would be a general movement from, for example, west to east, left to right, top to bottom.

Order of increasing importance. Order of increasing importance is preferable to the reverse since it helps to maintain interest and to give added weight to the most significant findings. Of course, this arrangement is only suitable where the findings do in fact vary in their importance.

Inductive. According to this arrangement essential data is presented at the beginning of the thesis. The general conclusions based on this data then follow in the order in which they were induced. This order is appropriate in theses which set out to describe a process of reasoning. The cause–effect arrangement is very similar.

Simple to complex, general to particular. In each of these arrangements the writer gives an overall picture in the earlier part of the thesis and then proceeds to deal with his subject in progressively greater detail.

Deductive. This is widely used in social science theses. The theses would contain the following parts in this order:

(i) Purpose of research, hypothesis to be tested.
(ii) Description of the collection of data (how the sample was selected, the information collected and analysed).
(iii) The data.
(iv) Relation of data to hypothesis.
(v) Conclusions. This would include comments on the value of research and references to inconclusive evidence. It may end with 'recommendations'.

Some social science journals have a similar standard arrangement which all articles submitted must follow.

Students writing reports based on survey work should familiarise themselves with the United Nations *Recommendations Concerning The Preparation of Reports of Sampling Surveys*, which covers content and organization. This publication is reproduced in full by Moser.*

4. Subdivisions

In long theses, the chapters are sometimes subdivided. Each section is numbered and has a heading. Subdivisions are helpful to the reader. They also make the student's writing task easier since the headings signpost the stages in the argument and consequently relieve the student of much of the task of maintaining continuity and achieving coherence by the use of transitional devices. However, many tutors object to subdivisions and students should find out their tutor's views on this matter. The student should also give some thought to the way in which the

---

* *Survey Methods in Social Investigation*, London, 1958, pp. 302–307.

headings are worded and also to how they are presented. In general, headings should be short and give a clear indication of the subject.

5. *Appendixes*

Appendixes are relatively short sections normally placed after the body of the thesis. They usually contain the following kinds of supporting material:

(a) Tables and figures too large or too detailed to be inserted in the body of the text without seriously affecting continuity. Appendixes are especially suitable where this material provides additional evidence rather than immediate clarification.

(b) Notes on the method of research used, especially when this information is rather too detailed or long for inclusion in a preface or introduction.

(c) Copies of questionnaires used in the research.

(d) Case studies too long for inclusion in the body of the text.

(e) Very long quotations.

(f) Copies of documents worth quoting because they are not easily available to the reader.

(g) The bibliography of a controversy.

(h) The bibliography of a little-known author.

(i) A list of non-written sources.

In each case the student must assure himself that the inclusion of the appendix is necessary. There may be a temptation to make appendixes of material that one is reluctant to discard. As always the criterion is relevance; superfluous appendixes detract from the value of the thesis.

6. *Arranging the Notes*

Once the student has decided on his organization he should arrange his notes in corresponding order. He will probably find it easier to write the thesis if he divides his notes into small manageable groups, each representing a division of a chapter or a stage in the argument.

'Training Chemical Engineering Graduates in Industry'
Outline

---

1. The training acts and the training boards
   (a) background to the act
   (b) its aims
   (c) the training boards
   (d) the engineering boards
2. Manpower requirements
   (a) policy for manpower in 1960s
   (b) supply of manpower in 1960s
   (c) factors affecting supply
   (d) the board and supply
3. University's supply of manpower
   (a) liaison with industry
   (b) university spending
   (c) problems with graduates
   (d) criticisms of courses
4. Qualifications needed in industry
   (a) value of the degree
   (b) routes to Chartered Engineer, etc.
   (c) types of training
   (d) career structure
5. A graduate's view of industry

Brian Steel (B. Sc. Econ. student, 3rd year)

---

7. *The Outline*

Once he has arranged the notes, the student should make a formal outline for the thesis. A formal outline is one in which each chapter is clearly headed and numbered and in which the subdivisions (or main points in each chapter) are indented and numbered. This kind of outline is useful to the student because it enables him to see the structure of his thesis at a glance. For the same reason it is useful to the tutor and, in many departments, students are required to submit formal outlines to their tutors before they produce a first draft.

VII

COMPOSITION

Before writing the first draft the student should supply himself with basic materials. Of these the most important is a large supply of writing paper; it is never wise to overcrowd a page and the student should allow plenty of space for corrections and for the insertion of additional material.

Since the notes embody the results of the research the thesis will obviously be based on them. By now the student should have rejected unwanted material and arranged the rest of the notes in the order in which he will use them in the thesis. As he writes he simply works his way through the notes, putting them aside as he progresses. If they have been arranged logically he should have no difficulty in linking them.

As was said in the previous chapter the writer will make his task easier if he divides the notes into manageable groups. Each one should represent either a main stage in the argument or a distinct part of the evidence and involve no more than a few hundred words. By dividing the writing task into separate stages the student will find it much easier and he can help himself maintain good progress by setting a date by which each part should be completed.

1. *Style*

A thesis must be reasonably well written. Before submitting it the student should make sure that it contains no errors of spelling, grammar or punctuation. He should also ensure that what he has written is clear and that his style is reasonably concise. Correctness, clarity and conciseness are the features of any good style. In addition, certain special qualities in the language and tone are distinctive of academic writing and the student ought to achieve these in his work.

Theses should be written in a formal style. Put very simply, this means the student must not write as though he were talking to a friend. He must not abbreviate or use exclamations nor must he use colloquialisms or slang. Normally he should write in complete sentences. In general he should avoid using personal pronouns and should employ sentence constructions which tend to emphasize the subject rather than the investigator; 'the conclusion was that . . . ' or 'the writer concluded that . . . ' is usually preferred to 'I concluded that . . . '. This is because the writer's style should convey the impression of impartiality and detachment rather than personal involvement. However, the student need not feel that he has to cultivate the excessively formal, rather pompous style that we have come to associate with the civil service.

The relationship that the writer establishes with the reader should be formal but it should also be courteous. It is one of the conventions of scholarly writing to draw attention to the originality of the research and the importance of the findings. However, the writer should not appear immodest or to be claiming too much for his findings. It would not be appropriate for him to conclude his thesis with the comment that it contained 'some of the most significant research yet carried out in this field'. He should leave such comments for the examiner!

Another danger is that the writer may appear to be condescending to his audience, if he assumes that they are totally ignorant of the subject under discussion. Theses are written for knowledgeable people and this should be reflected in the tone of the writing. For instance, the student should not spend too much space giving background information on his subject, nor should he make such remarks as 'the reader may not be aware that . . . ' or 'it is obvious that . . . '.

It is conventional to draw attention to any errors that one has found in the work of other researchers. Occasionally whole chapters are based on criticisms of earlier writers. Here it is important that the student should be courteous and not labour the faults of others.

Lastly, in general, humour is out of place in writing of this kind. The student may relate a humorous anecdote if it is relevant and he feels that it makes his point particularly well. However, he should take care not to let any facetiousness creep into his style.

2. *Quotations*

In Chapter III the circumstances were given in which the student would quote material rather than paraphrase or simply refer the reader to its source. Quotations tend to add interest to the text and can occasionally be used for this purpose alone. In general the student should beware of quoting too much or too often; a long series of quotations loosely strung together does not make a good thesis.

The best quotation is a short one. If it is four lines of prose or under it should be placed in the body of the text and enclosed in single quotation marks. For quotations within quotations, use double marks. Up to three lines of poetry can also be quoted in this way provided that a slash (/) is placed between lines. (Only the stuttering rifles' rapid rattle/Can patter out their hasty orisons.) Short quotations in the text can be introduced in one of the following ways:

Smith says that 'Britain is no longer a world power'.
As Smith says, 'Britain is no longer a world power'.
Smith says: 'Britain is no longer a world power'.

Longer quotations must be preceded by a colon, set off from the text and indented at least 20 mm. Quotation marks should not be used. Departments differ as to what they regard as short and long quotations. Some will permit more than four lines to be quoted in the body of the text, some less. The student must consult his tutor about this.

Quotations must be completely accurate. They must keep to the spelling and punctuation of the original but it is permissible to modernize the type. Any omissions or insertions must be indicated in the manner described in Chapter III. When writing the rough draft there is no need to copy quotations from the notes. The more often a quotation is transcribed the greater chance of making an error. Instead, the note can be pinned to the manuscript.

3. *Illustrative Material*

The term 'illustrative material' is used here to cover all tables, graphs, charts, diagrams, drawings, maps and photographs. The function of this material is to convey a piece of information more clearly and more concisely than it could be given in prose. Some material can only be presented effectively through such illustrations. Occasionally tables and maps incorporate primary information and provide a basis for discussion in the text; in other cases the illustrations may serve to supplement information in the text.

Nothing must be included in the thesis that is unnecessary. The writer must assure himself that any illustrative material he proposes to include will serve a genuinely useful purpose. Far from improving a thesis, irrelevant photographs and charts detract from its worth.

All tables, charts, graphs, maps and drawings should be made as simple and as clear as possible. Too much detail will make them difficult to understand. For example, it is better to compose two or more tables than to concentrate a large amount of information in one. Illustrations should not be cramped since this makes them difficult to follow.

All illustrative material must be clearly labelled and numbered. Different types of illustration should be separately numbered, the numbering being determined by the order in which they appear in the thesis: **Map 1, 2, 3; Table 1, 2, 3.** Later the student will have to provide each illustration with a title and compose lists of tables, maps, etc., for inclusion in the final version.

4. *Miscellaneous Points*

When a person's name is mentioned in the text it should be given in the form in which it normally appears: **T. S. Eliot** rather than **Thomas S. Eliot.**

Foreign words and phrases should be underlined except when they appear in quoted material.

The titles of books, journals, pamphlets and other separately published works (such as long poems) cited in the text and footnotes should be underlined. Parts of books, such as short poems, essays, journal articles, should be placed in quotation marks. Quotation marks should also be used for unpublished works such as theses.

Book titles that are very long can be given in an abbreviated form as long as this form is used consistently throughout the thesis.

Numbers under three digits should be spelt out but this is not necessary for figures of three digits or over or where figures are a major feature of the material.

In the case of inclusive numbers, the second number should be written in full up to 999: **750–757**. With larger numbers, if the second is within the same hundred, then only the last two figures need be given: **1945–51**. Otherwise the second figure should be written out in full: **1869–1904.**

Dates should never be spelt out. If a full date is given the order should be date number, month, year.

History students should remember that between 1582 and 1752 England continued to use the Julian Calender so that during that period English dates were eleven days behind those on the Continent. If the student is discussing both English and Continental dates in his thesis, then he should either convert English dates to the Gregorian Calender, notifying the reader of this in the preface or in an early footnote, or write all dates in the following manner: 1st/11th March, 8th/18th August.

During the same period, the new year in England began on 25th March. Dates between 1st January and 24th March can either be modernized or written in the following manner: **24th March, 1687–88, 1st January, 1687–92.** If the writer modernizes the dates he must draw the reader's attention to this fact in the preface or in an early footnote.

VIII

FOOTNOTES AND REFERENCES

1. *Types of Footnotes*

Footnotes are most usually used for the following purposes:

(a) To indicate the source of information (including a non-bibliographical source). The student *must* acknowledge the source of all quoted material, of facts obtainable from only one source, and of another writer's views or arguments. On the other hand, he need not give the source of proverbs or of information which is available from a wide variety of sources.
(b) To refer the reader to further sources of information on the subject under discussion.
(c) To refer the reader to another part of the thesis or to another footnote.
(d) To give information that clarifies something in the text of the thesis. This would include the explanation of foreign words and phrases, the conversion of unfamiliar kinds of money, etc.
(e) To give the original version of material that has been translated in the text.
(f) To present the other point of view on a subject which is a matter of minor controversy.
(g) To make a minor point that would interfere with continuity if it were made in the text.
(h) To elaborate upon or modify a point made in the text.

Some departments state that footnotes should be used only to acknowledge sources of information and for cross-references and that, in other cases, the material should either be included in the body of the text or expanded into an appendix. Students must, therefore, consult their tutor on the use of footnotes.

In the finished thesis these notes may appear at the end of the chapter or thesis or at the bottom of each page. In the former case the numbering will have to be continuous; in the latter it may begin anew on each page. The student will have to consult department regulations on this matter. In general, notes are placed at the bottom of the relevant page so that the reader is saved the trouble of constantly referring to another part of the thesis.

2. *References*

Some establishments ask their students to use the Harvard System of referencing. With this method the author's name, the publication date, and the page are given in the body of the text in brackets:

Another writer referred to this as 'an exploratory task' (Lawton, 1968, p. 77).

Where the student is using several publications by a single writer issued in the same year an abbreviated title should be given after the author's name. The reader uses this information to look up full details of the source in the bibliography. The advantage of this sytem is that it is simple and easy to use. Its disadvantage is that the reader has to refer constantly to the back of the thesis.

Perhaps for these reasons many establishments take the view that with a few exceptions, which we shall discuss, a reference should contain a full description of the source. This means reproducing all the details recorded on the source card together with the information concerning page numbers, etc., noted on the top right-hand corner of the note card:

3. Thomas Gray, *The Correspondence of Thomas Gray*, ed. Paget Toynbee and Leonard Whibley, Oxford, 1935, I, 48.

If your own supervisor takes this view, then it would be advisable for you to re-read Chapter III at this stage.

It is permissible to abridge these references in the following circumstances:

(a) Avoiding repetition. If some of the information, such as the author's name and the title, has been given in the text then this can be omitted from the reference so that the citation might read thus:

Cambridge, 1953, p. 27.

(b) Frequent references to one work. Some theses draw on a very large number of written sources. In these cases the student may wish to invent his own abbreviations for the books he cites most often. This is particularly useful if the title of publication details are very long. If he does this he must either include a key to the abbreviations at the beginning of his thesis or, alternatively, quote the full details in his first reference, indicating there the manner in which he will abbreviate them in following references. For examples of such abbreviations see page 79.

(c) References to well-known works. The titles of well-known works can usually be abbreviated:

Moser, *Survey Methods*, p. 53.

However, the student should beware of abridging the publication details (edition, publisher, date) since well-known works have often come out in several editions.

(d) Several citations within a short period. Where a work is cited on several occasions within a short period, it is permissible to abbreviate the second and subsequent references, provided there are few intervening references to other works and the space between each citation is not great (no more than two pages).

Where the references to one work are consecutive it is usually sufficient simply to give the page number:

1. Denis Lawton, *Social Class, Language and Education*, London, 1968, p. 23.
2. p. 24.
3. p. 31.

However, in these circumstances, many tutors insist on the use of 'ibid' (the same work) in the second and subsequent references: **ibid, p. 24.**

Where a reference to another work intervenes the author's name must be given:

1. **Denis Lawton**, *Social Class, Language and Education*, **London, 1968, p. 5.**
2. **C. A. Moser**, *Survey Methods in Social Investigation*, **London, 1958, p. 80.**
3. **Lawton, p. 8.**

Some authorities expect to see 'op. cit.' (the work previously referred to) used in these cases: **Lawton, op. cit., p. 8.** However, most tutors feel this abbreviation is unnecessary and often confusing. Ask your own tutor about this.

The author's name is probably sufficient if only one work or only one edition of a work by that person has been cited in the thesis. If more than one has been used then an abbreviated title will have to be given as well, e.g.

Lawton, *Social Class,* **p. 8.**

3. *Punctuation of References*

The purpose of inserting punctuation marks in references is to help the reader distinguish each item of information. There is no standard method of punctuation and tutors are usually content to let the student devise his own method, provided that it is clear and that he uses it consistently.

The simplest method of punctuation is to put a comma between each item of information. However, this is not very clear in cases where the information concerning publication is fairly detailed. For this reason some writers prefer to place all publication details (place, date) in parenthesis:

Survey Methods in Social Investigation **(London, 1958), p. 5.**

In any event if the county (or state) as well as the town is cited, then it is obviously desirable to use some mark other than a comma. The same problem arises when one wants to separate the main title from the subtitle. In both cases a colon is probably the best answer.

63

4. *Quotations in Footnotes*

Quotations in footnotes should be as short as possible and should not be set off from the rest of the note. The source should be given in brackets immediately after the author's name or, alternatively, after the quotation:

> **3. p. 55. Parsons and Hughes (*Written Communication for Business Students*, London 1970, p. 17) say that 'difficulties arise from ignorance'.**
>
> **3. p. 55. Parsons and Hughes say that 'difficulties arise from ignorance' (*Written Communication for Business Students*, London, 1970, p. 17).**

5. *Accuracy*

It is necessary to stress here that the details given in citation must be as complete as is necessary and accurate. Postgraduate students could easily be failed for inaccuracies and care is required at every level.

IX

FINAL PARTS

1. *Title Page*

The title page should include all of the following:

(a) The title of the thesis. This will normally have been registered with the tutor before the thesis is submitted. Titles should obviously give an immediate indication of the scope of the thesis. As a general rule they should be short; sometimes a short title is given followed by an explanatory subtitle.

(b) The course or degree for which the thesis is being submitted.

(c) The name of the establishment.

(d) The department or faculty in which the work was carried out (not always required).

(e) The (month and) year of submission.

(f) The name of the student.

2. *Table of Contents*

A table of contents must be drawn up and included at the beginning of the thesis. The table should give accurately the titles and commencing page of all chapters, major subdivisions and appendixes. It should also include the commencing page of the preface, the bibliography and each of the lists of abbreviations, tables and figures if these appear in the thesis. The page should be stated on the right of the page. See pages 77–78 for examples.

3. *Acknowledgements*

If the student received help in, for example, the provision of facilities or owes a special debt to a particular source, this should be acknowledged in a Preface, Foreword or a section entitled Acknowledgements.

4. *Abstract*

Some establishments require theses to be provided with an abstract. An abstract is a summary of the thesis. The regulations usually stipulate its maximum length; this is most frequently 300 words but can be as much as 600 depending on the length of thesis. The abstract should indicate the main points that emerge during the course of the thesis and the conclusions. Most establishments require the abstract to be bound with the thesis but a few prefer it to be submitted separately. Some universities publish abstracts in annual volumes.

5. *List of Abbreviations*

If the student has invented abbreviations for works to which he refers frequently in the text a key to these must be provided at the beginning of the thesis and should be presented in the manner shown on page 79.

6. *Lists of Tables and Figures*

Tables and Figures must be listed separately. The list of tables normally precedes that of figures.

7. *Headings and Subdivisions*

These should give a clear indication of content and be as short as possible. Number chapters and appendixes in upper-case roman numerals; for subdivisions, use arabic numerals and, to list points, small letters. All illustrative material should be provided with headings, titles or captions.

8. *List of References*

If the references have not been included at the bottom of the appropriate page, or at the end of each chapter, they should be listed at the end of the thesis immediately after the appendixes.

9. *List of Non-written Sources*

An appendix containing an alphabetical list of people, places and organizations should be included at the end of thesis, embodying the results of field work. Students must remember to be consistent in their method of description. If this list takes the form of an appendix it should be placed with other appendixes immediately after the main part of the thesis.

10. *The Bibliography*

A bibliography is a list of written sources consulted during the course of research. All works cited in the text and footnotes are normally included. On occasions the list may also include works that the student found useful in formulating ideas presented in the thesis; the student should consult his tutor as to what should be included in the bibliography. The bibliography can either be organized as a single alphabetical list or divided into two or more lists in one of the following ways:

(a) Unpublished/published sources. MS theses are classified as 'unpublished' works.
(b) Primary/secondary sources. See page 13 for the distinction. Primary works are those that receive the greatest attention in the thesis. In a thesis on *Hamlet* Eliot's essay on the play would be a secondary source; in a thesis on Eliot's critical writings the same essay would be a primary source.
(c) Books/articles.
(d) Division by chapter. This is appropriate where different sources have been used for each chapter.

Some methods of presenting the bibliography involve a combination of these arrangements. The student should consult his tutor on the ones that are acceptable in the department. When the student has decided how the bibliography is to be organized he should arrange the source cards accordingly. The information in each entry is written out in the same order in which it was recorded on the source card, except that the author's surname is normally placed before his initials. Students using the Harvard

System should note that, according to this method, the date is placed between the author's name and the title of the publication:

Lawton, Denis, 1968, *Social Class, Language and Education*, **London.**

X

EDITING THE FIRST DRAFT

Once the thesis has been typed and bound only minor mistakes and omissions can be corrected. Therefore it is essential for the student to edit his work carefully before he hands it to a typist. He should ask himself the following questions since these are the criteria the examiners will have in mind when they come to assess the thesis:

1. *Content*

(a) Does the thesis fulfil the aims stated in the preface (or introduction)?
(b) Have the major conclusions been persuasively argued?
(c) Is there enough material in the thesis to support the claims made?
(d) Is all the material in the thesis relevant?
(e) Is the research on which the thesis is based sufficiently extensive?
(f) How certain is the reliability of the major sources?
(g) Are all the quotations, tables, maps, etc. accurate?
(h) Is the technical information up to date?
(i) Are the citations and cross-references accurate?
(j) Are the bibliographical details complete and correct?
(k) Does the table of contents give an accurate indication of what the thesis contains? Make sure that the items in the table are identical to the headings in the text.

2. *Form and Arrangement*

(a) Are all the elements of the thesis present—title page, table of contents, lists of tables and illustrations, appendixes and bibliography?

(b) Has the thesis introductory and concluding sections?
(c) Is the arrangement of the chapters and the material within the chapters logical?

3. *Style*

(a) Does the language conform to prevailing standards of usage? Check grammar, spelling and punctuation. Make sure that the punctuation in footnotes and in the bibliography is consistent.
(b) Is what you have written clear? Make sure you have not assumed too much knowledge in your reader.
(c) Have you expressed your findings and arguments concisely?
(d) Is the style coherent? Check that you have made the best possible use of transitional devices.
(e) Is the tone of the thesis courteous? Make sure that you have nowhere condescended to the reader. Look again at your references to the work of other writers to make sure that they could not cause offence.

XI

TYPING AND BINDING

Good presentation is important and, if the student is not himself a competent typist, he should give his manuscript to someone who has some experience in typing theses and who is familiar with accepted conventions. Many establishments issue instructions on these matters and the student should obtain a copy of them.

1. *Paper*

For both original and carbon copies use good quality paper of International A4 size. Type on only one side of the page. The copy paper must not be so thin that it is transparent. Use black carbon paper and remember to replace it frequently. Students must consult the relevant regulations on the number of copies to be submitted.

2. *Margins*

A margin of not less than 40 mm should be allowed on the left-hand side of the page to allow for binding, and at least 20 mm on the right. About 20 mm should be left at the top and bottom of the page.

3. *Spacing*

The text of the thesis should be double-spaced but indented quotations and footnotes should be single-spaced.

4. *Dividing Words*

Do not divide words of one syllable. Normally divide words at the end of a syllable. Do not divide a word at the end of a page.

5. Headings and Titles

Chapter headings should be capitalized (ORIGINS) and centred. They can be typed on a separate page or at the top of the page on which the text commences. Subdivision headings should be typed from the left-hand margin in lower-case type and underlined. A major subdivision should normally be commenced on a new page. The titles of appendixes should be capitalized and centred on the page on which the text commences. The titles of tables and charts should also be capitalized, centred, and placed above the material to which they refer. Captions to photographs should be capitalized and centred; they may be placed below.

6. Tables, Graphs, and Diagrams

Tables should be placed as near as possible to that part of the text to which they refer. If the table is fairly short it can be included in the body of the text. In this case the table number (TABLE 3) should be separated from the text by two or three spaces. Two spaces below, the heading should be typed in capitals. If an explanatory note to the table is necessary an asterisk should be used; if several are needed use small letters. The notes themselves should be placed immediately below the table, and not with the other footnotes at the bottom of the page. If the writer is quoting the table, the source should be indicated below the table preceded by the word 'Source'. If any explanatory notes to the table are the student's they should be placed *below* the name of the source. If the notes are part of the quotation, they should be placed *above* the source. Lengthy tables should be placed in appendixes.

If two sheets of paper need to be joined together to form the chart, an adhesive should be used such as Scotch Brand Magic 810.

If material needs to be folded make each fold as wide as possible but take care to leave at least three-quarters of an inch on the left-hand side. Fold in such a way that the last fold is turned upwards.

Very large charts, maps, etc., may be placed in a pocket at the end of the thesis or submitted in a separate container but, in general, all illustrative material should be bound in with the thesis.

7. *Photographs*

Photographs may have a glazed or matt finish. Some departments prefer the former. Whatever one's choice one should be consistent. Black and white photographs should be mounted on cartridge or bond paper, never on copy paper. A paste should be used rather than gum or glue. Corners should be used for colour photographs as gum or glue may affect the colouring. Captions to photographs can be placed above or below. Above is preferable if there are notes to the photograph and an indication of source. If the photograph is set sideways the bottom of the photograph and the caption should be on the right of the page. In all cases allow 40 mm on the left and 20 mm on the right and at the top and bottom of the page.

8. *Footnotes*

Footnote numbers in the text should be placed immediately after the relevant material and slightly (not one space) above the line. If the footnotes themselves are set at the bottom of each relevant page at least four spaces should be left between the bottom of the text and the footnotes. In addition, some establishments prefer a separating line to be typed part or all of the way across the page two spaces below the text. The footnotes themselves should be singled-spaced and punctuated as the example illustrates.

9. *Bibliography*

The heading 'Bibliography' should be capitalized and centred. The headings of subdivisions (e.g. *Primary Sources*) should be typed in lower-case from the left margin and underlined. Two spaces should separate the division heading and the first entry in the division. Each entry should begin from the left margin but the second and subsequent lines of an entry should be indented four or five spaces and single-spaced. Where more than one work by the same author is cited it is usual to type a line instead of his name in the second and subsequent entries.

10. *Pagination*

Some establishments require the thesis to be paginated continuously in arabic numerals; others prefer the use of a small roman for prefactory material, starting the arabic numerals on the first page of the body of the thesis. Consult your tutor on this matter. In either case it is usual to place the number at the centre of the bottom of the page.

11. *Corrections*

Before sending the thesis to a binder the student should re-read it to correct any typing errors. Some establishments permit small errors of punctuation and spelling to be corrected in ink but if there are several errors on a page it should certainly be retyped. If a thesis is submitted with errors it will probably be returned to the student for correction before it is finally accepted.

12. *Binding*

Some establishments require theses to be bound. Students must consult department regulations concerning the way in which the thesis is to be bound; usually the establishment will have the name of a local firm of binders who undertake this work and are familiar with the establishment's requirements. On the spine it is usual to have the course, the year in which the thesis is examined, and the initials and surname of the student. Many establishments also require this information, together with the title of the thesis, to be placed on the front cover. Binders do not undertake the work of collating the thesis and the student should make sure the pages are in the correct order before copies are sent to the binder.

13. *Sample Pages*

To illustrate conventional layout, there follow some sample pages taken from dissertations:

RADLEY COLLEGE OF TECHNOLOGY

Department of Business Studies

B.Sc. Economics Dissertation

'Training Engineering Graduates in Industry'
by
David Lewis

1970

THE EARLY BROWNING

(1812–1840)

A thesis submitted for the degree of

Doctor of Philosophy

in the University of London

by

SAMUEL JOHN HUGHES

1966

CONTENTS

CONTENTS

ABBREVIATIONS

Duff
David Duff, An Exposition of Browning's 'Sordello' with Historical and Other Notes, London, 1906.

Forster Pauline
Robert Browning, Pauline, London, 1833. This copy is in the Forster-Dyce Collection in the Victoria and Albert Museum and contains MS notes by Browning and J. S. Mill.

Griffin & Minchin
W. Hall Griffin and Harry Christopher Minchin, The Life of Robert Browning, 3rd edition, London, 1938.

Hayward
J. W. von Goethe, Faust: A Dramatic Poem, trans. A. Hayward, 2nd edition, London, 1834.

Herford
C. H. Herford, Robert Browning, London, 1905.

Hood
Letters of Robert Browning Collected by Thomas J. Wise, ed. Thurman L. Hood, London, 1933.

Hovelaque
Henri-Léon Hovelaque, La Jeunesse de Robert Browning, Paris, 1932.

Letters
The Letters of Robert Browning and Elizabeth Barrett, 1845-1846, 2 vols, London, 1899.

Lounsbury
Thomas R. Lounsbury, The Early Literary Career of Robert Browning, London, 1912.

Pottle
Frederick A. Pottle, Shelley and Browning: A Myth and Some Facts, Chicago, 1923.

8

TABLES

10

things (as Dutchman do cheese) the better for being mouldy and worm-eaten.[1]

He loves 'musty things . . . raked from dunghills.'[2] Samuel Butler described him in very similar terms:

> He is an old frippery-Philosopher, that has so strange a natural Affection to worm-eaten Speculation that it is apparent he has a Worm in his Skull.[3]

Oldmixon said that the work of antiquarians was reserved for 'those, whose Minds, like barren Soils, will never bear without dunging'[4]; antiquarians ' . . . hope like the Cock to find a Jewel in the Dunghill.'[5] Pope's Cornelius Scriblerus is based upon the popular conception of the antiquarian. In the book, Scriblerus becomes infuriated because the rust has been cleaned off an old shield:

> . . . where, where is the beautiful Crust that cover'd thee so long? where those Traces of Time, and Fingers as it were of Antiquity? Where all those beautiful obscurities . . .[6]

Not long after, Chesterfield advised his correspondent not to read the works of antiquarians: 'Let blockheads read what blockheads wrote.'[7]

---

[1] Microcosmography, ed. Harold Osborne, London, 1933, p. 21.
[2] p. 21.
[3] Characters and Passages from Notebooks, ed. A. R. Waller, Cambridge, 1908, p. 42.
[4] An Essay on Criticism, London, 1728, p. 78.
[5] p. 78.
[6] Memoirs of the Extraordinary Life, Works and Discoveries of Martin Scriblerus, London, 1741, p. 20.
[7] Letters of Philip Dormer Stanhope, 4th Earl of Chesterfield, ed. Bonamy Dobrée, London, 1932, IV, 1597.

54

Gooch, G. P., History and Historians in the Nineteenth Century, 2nd edition, London, 1952.

Grant, Michael, Roman Literature, Cambridge, 1954.

Gray, Thomas, The Correspondence of Thomas Gray, ed. Paget Toynbee and Leonard Whibley, 3 vols, Oxford, 1935.

Green, Matthew, A Comparative View of the State and Faculties of Man with Those of the Animal World, London, 1765.

Grynaeus, Simon, De Legendae Historiae, Basle, 1576.

Hales, John, Golden Remains, of the Ever Memorable Mr. John Hales, of Eaton-College, London, 1673.

Ham, Roswell G., 'Dryden as Historiographer-Royal: The Authorship of "His Majesties Declaration Defended",' RES, XI, July, 1935, 284-298.

Hanson, Laurence, The Government and the Press 1695-1763, London, 1936.

Hardy, Thomas Duffus, Syllabus (in English) of the Documents Relating to England and Other Kingdoms Contained in the Collection Known as 'Rymer's Foedera', London, 1869.

Harte, Walter, An Essay on Satire, Particularly on the Dunciad, London, 1730.

Havens, Raymond D., 'Simplicity, a Changing Concept,' JHI, XIV, January 1953, 3-32.

Hayley, William, An Essay on History; In Three Epistles to Edward Gibbon, Esq., With Notes, London, 1780.

Hayward, John, The History of the Life and Raigne of Henry the Fourth, King of England, London, 1642.

——, The Life and Raigne of King Edward the Sixt, London, 1630.

234

XII

THE VIVA VOCE

In many establishments the students will have to attend a formal interview (sometimes called a 'viva voce' or simply a 'viva') based on the thesis. The interview panel will probably include the student's Head of Department and other members of staff, and may also include external examiners from other colleges.

This interview has several purposes:

(a) To establish the authenticity of the thesis. It is not unknown for students to submit theses which are not their own work and one of the purposes of the viva is to establish that the student has in fact carried out the research described in the thesis. To this end he may be questioned closely on parts of the thesis.

(b) To test the student's knowledge of areas surrounding his subject but relevant to it.

(c) To elicit more information about the techniques of research employed.

(d) To ask the student to expand upon points made in the thesis which need explanation or clarification.

(e) To provide the student with detailed criticisms of the thesis. A thesis may be acceptable and yet still have faults. The examiners may wish to take this opportunity to point them out, especially if the student is known to be considering any further research in this field.

To prepare for the interview the student should re-read his thesis. Whilst he does so he should try to anticipate any points the examiners are likely to make. What defences could be offered for this? How could that part be expanded? What other sources could be mentioned in connection with this point? What shortcomings does he now see in the thesis which he might want to draw to the attention of the examiners? Try to look at the thesis from the point of view of the external examiner. What deficiencies is he likely to notice?

Apart from re-reading the thesis closely there is very little the student can do to prepare for the oral examination. All that remains is for him to get a good night's sleep and to ensure that on the day he is punctual and smartly dressed.

During the interview the student should pay some attention to his demeanour; the way in which one enters a room and sits in a chair contribute to the examiner's impression of a student. All questions should be answered as fully and as clearly as possible. Throughout the interview the student should try to give the air of being confident and relaxed. At the same time, however, he should be prepared to defer to the examiners where necessary.

For the student who has carried out his research well and presented the results carefully, the oral examination should present few problems. By this stage he should know more about his topic than his tutors and, in many cases, the interview turns out to be a pleasant exchange between people who share an interest in the same field. The progress of students in most establishments is closely supervised and tutors usually try to ensure that the thesis is an acceptable standard before it is ever seen by the examiners. Consequently, few students fail in the oral examination. For this reason alone one hopes that the student who has followed the instructions in this book will have few reasons to worry.

BIBLIOGRAPHY

In preparing this book the author made use of the following publications to which the student is referred for further information on various aspects of project work:

British Standards Institution, *British Standard* 1629: *Bibliographical References*, London, 1950.

Hart, Horace, *Rules for Compositors and Readers at the University Press Oxford*, 37th edition, London, 1967.

Madge, John, *The Tools of Social Science*, London, 1953.

Mann, Peter H., *Methods of Sociological Enquiry*, Oxford, 1968.

Moser, C. A. *Survey Methods in Social Investigation*, London, 1958.

Parker, William Riley, *The M.L.A. Style Sheet*, 2nd edition, New York, 1970.

Turabian, Kate L., *A Manual for Writers of Term Papers, Theses and Dissertations*, 3rd edition, Chicago, 1967.

INDEX

abbreviations, 22, 23, 24, 29, 59, 62–63
abbreviations in thesis, list of, 48, 66, 79
abstracting services, 34, 35
abstract in thesis, 48, 66
acknowledgements in thesis, 48, 65–66
action research, 42
Acts of Parliament, references to, 25
anon, 23
anonymous works in references, 23
appendixes in theses, 11, 48, 52, 60, 67, 69
articles, references to: collections, 23, 24; encyclopedias, 23, 24; serial publications, 24
Aslib Directory, 36
associations, 37
attitude surveys, 44
audience for thesis, 48, 56
author's name in references, 22–23, 24, 25, 61–63
autobiographies, 37

Bagley, William A., 33
Besterman, Theodore, 34
Bible, references to, 29
Bibliographic Index, 34
bibliographies, 32–38
Bibliographies Subject & National, 33
bibliography in thesis, 11, 14, 21, 48, 67, 69, 73, 82
binding the thesis, 11, 14, 74
biographies, 33
brackets, square, 22, 30
British Museum, 18, 37
British National Bibliography, 34
British Standards, 8, 24, 85
British Union-Catalogue of Periodicals, 35

cameras, hidden, 42
cantos, references to, 29

Chandler, G., 33
charts in theses, 72
circulation lists, 40
citations, see 'references'
classics, references to, 23
Collison, Robert L., 33
conclusion to thesis, 49–50
colloquialisms, 56
columns, references to, 29
committees, 37
copies of thesis, number of, 11, 71
corrections to thesis, 74
correctness in language, 55, 70
correspondence, 37
councils, 37
county records, 36
courtesy in thesis writing, 56, 70
cross-references, 60
Cumulative Book Index, 34
Current British Directories, 37, 40

data processing, 46
dates in theses, 59
deadlines, 15, 55
diagrams in theses, 58, 72
diaries, 13, 37
dictionaries, 19, 32
directories, 33, 37, 40
Directory of British Associations, 37
dissertations, 35
documentation, see 'bibliography' and 'references'
drawings in theses, 58

ed, 23
edition in references, 23, 62
editor in references, 23
edn, 23
electoral registers, 40
ellipsis, 30
encyclopedias, 19, 33

TUTOR'S INSTRUCTIONS